Authority

A primer to political thought

By Malcolm Ramsey

To order additional copies of this book, contact:
Xlibris Corporation
1-888-795-4274
www.Xlibris.com
Orders@Xlibris.com
110762

Table of Contents

Part 1   *Introduction*

I admire and applaud the brave crusaders who try to influence, through protests people with authority. Environmental groups such as the David Suzuki Foundation, Green Peace, The Nature Conservancy and social justice groups namely the Occupy Movement bravely struggle to influence authority. These are the true heroes in our society. Numerous excellent documentaries, like Leonardo Dicaprio's 'The Eleventh Hour' and Al Gore's 'An Inconvenient Truth,' point out what will happen to our biosphere if we don't change course. However, when push comes to shove it's all very well to be informed about a problem but in today's world being informed is a useless exercise because individuals have no authority to do anything about it. My thesis offers a possible solution by empowering individuals giving them full citizenship, responsibility, and ownership in these problems. This authority would empower citizens to exercise their authority by demanding truth and expelling ineffectiveness.

Perhaps you've, watched such documentaries, read books or attended lectures about our ancestors to gain a tiny understanding of what it would be like to live in a world where there is no law against manslaughter, nonconsensual sex or genocide. It's not hard to believe that the most dangerous, cunning and cruel creature on the planet is not the shark but mankind. Some say we are nature's knives, put here to reduce the number of species on the planet. We are not only the most dangerous predator on the planet, but also the only predator of our own species. Our very success has come from this complicated survival strategy of killing our fellow man (murder) and having non-consensual sex (rape) to select the most intelligent beauties to reproduce. It's quite natural for the Serbian soldiers to kill the men of a village then lock up the women to be used as sex slaves. Such practices were common for great warriors such as the Ottomans, Genghis Khan and the standard among ancient as well as modern aggressors. The best incentive to fight hard was the sex at the end of the battle. Our political system is our only defense against our potential malevolence. Politics gives us rules protecting ourselves from ourselves. At the beginning of the third millennia the beautiful intelligent people who occupy the biosphere of this planet, the end product of thousands of generations of manslaughter and nonconsensual sex, are responsible for maintaining this law and order. We know if we work together we can save the biosphere and in so doing save thousands of future generations of our own species. The solution to a stable world is inevitable. Are you ready?

Political Questions

Living in a western civilization we can smugly look out the windows of our homes and marvel at a world filled with social justice, peace, security, an overabundance of goods and, hopefully joy. At the beginning of the Twenty-first century we can without doubt thank our system of politics for these blessings, however much as a prosperous man might worry about the loss of his wealth, should we not worry about losing these wonders?

Our addiction to injecting hydrocarbons into the arteries of our civilization is long past any chance of an easy withdrawal. Our collective conscious knows such indulgences are wrong but as a group we are unable to create effective change. There is overwhelming evidence in our recorded history to support the notion that politics plays the largest role in supporting and maintaining the quality of our lives, yet in western democracies our collective consciences play such a small part in the decisions made by our political system. Surely there is a way to increase the political participation of our citizens without disrupting the fine political balance we've achieved in the western world.

Unfortunately representative (participatory) democracy in western society is cumbersome and ineffectual. Representative democracy does not have the authority to make the changes necessary to bring our world into equilibrium. It seems everyone knows we have many serious problems urgently needing repairs but all we get from our political system is talk, while the taxpayer pays billions to protect ineffectual speechmakers.

There is something we can do; however, some would consider the political changes I am suggesting radical and my chances of attaining my goal are about the same as asking the entire population of western civilization to stand on their collective heads and walk around on its hands. I agree - the changes would be a radical shift in our thinking. However, is it possible that politically we are upside down, standing on our heads and walking around on our hands and all I'm doing is proposing politicians stand on their feet? Some might find standing on their heads and walking around on their hands easy, because from birth they have been doing just that. You can find them shuffling around the houses of governments. They have nice flat spots on the tops of their thick skulls to rest on, huge pecs, giant arms to move with and unfeeling thick-callused hands. Most of us find it hard to stand on our heads even if we have a wall to balance against. We get terrible headaches and can't see very far. From a political perspective I would like to point out that

"I think it would be better to stand on your feet."

it is better to stand on our feet. Individuals can stand on their feet, it's much more comfortable, we can see a long way in the distance, we don't get terrible headaches, and we can use our hands for more useful things.

This writing is not about parliamentary, institutional or electoral reform, it is about political franchise or suffrage. The fundamental principle of democracy is; **"each citizen possess exactly the same amount of political authority from the age of consent until the end of life."** There are many what-if scenarios and this is one of them. What if the people who live in western democracies demanded suffrage like their ancestors in the early part of the Twentieth Century? Ralph Nader, in his book, <u>Only the super rich can save us</u>, asks the question "what if the superrich financed reform fixing the government, returning power to the people, galvanized a movement for alternative forms of energy and advancing clean elections?" I applaud Ralph Nader's work; but I want to add one unlikely yet very vital aspect to this solution. We can fix the problems, but we all must be a part of the solution not just the superrich.

After the first great war of the Twentieth century the landless soldiers of British Empire returned with the argument that if they were good enough to die for the King they should be good enough to vote for a political representative. These disfranchised men, returning from the war were given the vote. The women of America and England who had been fighting for political franchise for decades, in the suffragette movement, were granted the right to vote for a representative soon after. We have a better world today because our ancestors had the courage to stand up to the authorities and demand their rights. In my opinion it is time to take up the call for a new suffrage. This time we will fight for our political franchise, the future of our children and equal say in the decisions made by our governments. Our political franchise is worth fighting for; if we win, there will be no more war, our economies will stabilize, we will be able to stop the destruction of our environment and our improved social structure will allow us to live happy fulfilling lives free of fear or oppression. Of course, there will be unforeseen positive consequences; for example, in Puerto Alegre Brazil, where for more than a decade an experiment with participative democracy has been going on, health care costs have gone down by thirty percent. I would also expect the cost of civil services and policing over time would decline because of the healthier population and shrinking crime rates.

Any change in our political system should be expected to take generations as it can only be accomplished through the population's acceptance of the new set of values and understandings. On one hand to rush into any change in our political system would not only harm future potential growth, but also destabilize our present system that is filled with checks and balances that work. On the other hand, if we can't get the superrich to support the needed democratic change, and if we wait too long, we'll be lost in another totalitarian society run by politically engineered corporations who are increasingly using modern communication tools to control the population. The most important thing is **to begin;** we must give the people of the world; **time** to do a well thought out job of reforming our decision-making mechanisms.

Step Back and Take a Look at *The Big Picture*

There is good evidence to support the idea that over the last three billion years successive waves of life have populated the biosphere of earth, a layer so thin and fragile in relation to the size of the planet. If you were really big, I'm talking huge, not just big assed big, but massive, standing beside the globe looking at the surface you wouldn't be able to detect mountains. The world would be glassy smooth. If you tried to touch the surface, the devastation on earth would probably not heal for 1000s of years, not to mention you'd probably burn your finger as you entered the outer atmosphere. If you pushed hard on the surface you'd realize the earth's crust is as thick as a water balloons', filled with liquid magma with an iron pit. Between the crust and the outer atmosphere there is a layer approximately eight kilometers thick, much thinner than a piece of cellophane stretched over a basketball, where all the living creatures on earth live. It's so thin you wouldn't be able to detect it without the use of a high-powered microscope.

If you were an extraterrestrial being looking down, you might notice some unusual discoloration around

London, New York or Tokyo, but for the most part you'd only see ocean, land and cloud. After viewing the planet with a powerful microscope you might come to the realization that the slug like creatures that move along the roads are the machines of an even smaller creatures, a species of primate that on closer inspection occupies the entire planet.

These primates seem to have unending energy to grind up the surface of the planet using energy they derive by digging up ancient carbon deposits and burning them in their machines. If you studied the planet for long enough, you'd realize this transformation was very unusual, and because it was happening at an ever-increasing rate, some sort of outcome to bring the planet back to equilibrium would happen in the near future. How exciting to be the scientist who just happened to be studying this planet at the ideal time to witness this event.

When it comes to trying to grasp the amount of time the planet has existed, relative to the life of a human, you might just as well give up. If we think man has existed for perhaps one million years, and we consider one generation to be twenty years, then you have fifty thousand generations. Few of us know much about the last three generations of our own families.

How much are we supposed to know about this speck of dust we call home related to the mass of our galaxy or the tiny spec our galaxy is relative to the universe? Yes, this thin layer, on this obscure planet, this biosphere, is where we evolved, where we live, and where we will always live. This place where a storm can be seen traveling across the surface of the planet at a snail's pace, where the fastest animals, birds, take a year to migrate over half of the planet, where some believe the first people to occupy the Americas took a thousand years to migrate from the far North to the far distant south of South America. We are living in the blink of an eye and the question is, do we have the intelligence to grasp the big picture and maintain this paradise, this thin biosphere, on this tiny planet?

It's difficult, if not impossible, to go beyond our lifetime of understandings; our prejudices, our religious beliefs. Many of these beliefs are so imbedded in the minds of some as to exploit our paradise to make it unlivable. Is there some way to control this out of control primate, the most dangerous, cunning and lethal creature to ever occupy this precious little space in the biosphere of this tiny planet? In my mind there's only one possibility- **politics**.

Most of us, at the thought of politics, feel quite ill, a kind of nausea, where we feel oppressed and hopeless. Something we would rather ignore if at all possible. It's like trying to walk with your hands and stand on your head. It causes headaches and makes you feel sick.

How would you like to live in a world where you hold politics as the dearest thing in your life, an institution you cherish, an institution that connects you to a world you love, a world where you have ownership, a place, and responsibility? Can you imagine a place where your dearest friends are politicians, standing with you, respected leaders in society, who you can trust to work for the betterment of all?

It seems the average citizen of today has a different opinion. I've heard politicians described as untrustworthy scumbag exploiters of the common man. The governments they participate in are shrouded in secrecy to protect their dishonesty. The sentiment is that politicians are not particularly intelligent people; they seem unaware of the consequences of the decisions they are making. Decisions that unknowingly lower the quality of life of the average citizen while compromising future life on this planet. Is it true many of the decisions made by politicians are made to satisfy their lust for power and wealth? Are elections popularity contests, filled with spin and sentiment, rather than a process to select good people to rule? Is there something wrong with our political system and can we fix it?

Few read the writings of modern political scientists or political philosophers, probably because the ideas found in their writings are too tiresome. If you do read them I think you'll find they almost exclusively write from the tangible, or realist perspective, carefully referencing their work from earlier works. All the potent ideas from the past are buried in the propaganda generated by the prejudices and fears of the great warlord heroes we read about in our history books.

Political Scientists are very good historians, they are first-class at accounting for and speculating on the outcomes in political competitions, but when it comes to finding answers to improving our political system, they leave that to the radicals and the revolutionaries. If we were talking about any other branch of science, we would find engineers or accountants who come up with new ideas, new ways of doing things, and new technologies based on the fundamental principles generated by scientists. Just imagine if we only had physicists and mathematicians but no engineers to design and build our roads and bridges. Engineers know how much steel and concrete is needed to build the center span of a bridge, they also know how to efficiently move traffic. Physicists and scientists don't have a clue about building bridges or roads just as political scientists know nothing about building a democratic political system but in both cases the foundation of understanding comes from the scientists. In political science there is a noticeable absence of engineers. Just imagine what our free market economy would be like if we only had economist and no accountants. If we had no engineers and used 200-year-old roads and bridges traffic would move slowly, it wouldn't flow efficiently and the old roads and bridges would probably collapse under the weight of our modern world. Is this not what's happening with modern politics? Why don't we have political engineers?

It's beyond comprehension to think the last real change in politics happened a few hundred years ago with the formation of the American Republic. Why are we so afraid to change our political systems? Wouldn't it be ideal if we had political engineers who could build roads and bridges of communication that would give the silent majority with its intelligence and common sense a role in decision-making? Political engineers could build mechanisms to smoothly bring forward the best solutions to resolve problems in our communities, in a process of moving towards consensus. Where are our political engineers?

How pleased are you with the decisions of your government? Do you feel you participate in the decisions your government makes? Do you feel elections are popularity contests having little to do with decisions made by government? Do you hear your fellow citizens criticizing and complaining about government decisions, always using the expression "they should do this or they should do that"?

We (I will always try to use the word, "we" not "they") can and will change our politics, always moving towards sustainability in our environment, our social structure and our economy.

Authority

Authority; a word from Roman law (Latin: auctoritas) is often replaced with the word power or political power. Both attempt to bring human beings together to work towards a common end; however, they differ in the question of legitimacy. The concept of authority has far reaching uses in all aspects of human life. A person can have intellectual authority as a medical doctor or with a PhD from an accredited university. High-ranking religious individuals have religious authority just as the leaders of environmental and human rights groups have moral authority.

Nature is filled with order resulting from natural authority relying on an imposed co-operation between species. Naturally we think of authority as having power over another. Because of the nature of man, this authority over another usually means oppression. When a right wing government is elected, the authority of the right-wing government oppresses the left-wing opposition. When you work under the authority of a boss, you are oppressed. At a different level a dictator oppresses his citizens with fear and intimidation. In our modern world, with few exceptions, we are all oppressed. If we are in charge, the taxman or the next level of authority oppresses us. Man's full potential can only come from, what some call liberty, the opposite of oppression. We need liberty in all aspects of life.

Some corporations have recognized the improved effect of giving their employees autonomy in their work places by using modern participative management techniques. Unfortunately, most of those companies don't headquarter in America, but rather Japan or other new democracies where change is still possible. It's not hard to see how successful they are by looking at the brands of automobiles on our roads.

Aristotle noted that people want to be left alone to go about their lives without interference. The problem being, people going about their lives usually interfere with others. This is where politics comes in; we need the authority of rules and regulations to minimize oppression, and we need government to make these rules using all of us as sources of authority. Let's challenge ourselves to reduce oppression in all levels of society.

For the sake of simplicity consider authority to have four natural levels. Let's use the words: cosmos, bios, demos, and ethnos to describe these levels.

The Authority of the Cosmos;

(The COSMOS: an orderly or harmonious system) Pythagoras first used the word perhaps to describe the starry firmament of the sky. In this case we will use cosmos in an ethereal way, perhaps we can think of it as another dimension or a parallel universe. If we can't find the answer to a question like what happens after we die let's use the cosmos as a place to explain it.

The cosmos is the highest level of authority. This is where the ancient Gods lived and controlled the Bios (nature). These ancient Gods controlled the wind, the rain; they brought plagues and orchestrated the building or destruction of great empires. The cosmos is a place where the dead lived on the other side of the river Styx. It's where the stars and the planets roamed until in modern times astronomers removed the heavenly bodies from the cosmos through research.

Today religions can be found which have divided the cosmos into heaven and hell. Heaven is where God and his son live, this is where the Buddhists go after they are enlightened (Nirvana) and the Muslims go to Mohamed and mix with Allah in paradise. Deep inside every conscious there is a cosmos, a place to explain death. Nothing has more authority than death to the human soul. When a person holds a gun to your head they have the ultimate authority over you, the authority of the Cosmos. The authority of our ancestors comes from the cosmos and upon birth we are all given a ticket to return.

The Authority of the Bios.

The authority of the bios is the authority of all living things. It is spring flowers bursting open exposing their sex to probing insects; it is early morning red blood cells pulsing through the arteries of a jogger running down a city street; it is chloroplasts poised to move with the gentle light of sunrise on a cool spring morning and it is birds shouting out their song of love in the early morning dampness. We call it the balance of nature, the struggle for survival. Placed before us undisturbed by man it passes our understanding of order. To understand the power of the Bios consider the love between a man and women and the authorities people will trample to fulfill their love. Shakespeare described this authority in his play Romeo and Juliet where two young lovers defy the authority of their tribes, the Capulets and the Montagues, to be together. Consider the drive to survive, to eat, to reproduce. Compare the mating behavior of humans to other animals; the joy we get from dressing up and adorning ourselves with what some would call war paint; how we love to go to parties and flaunt our beauty like preening birds. All these activities are part of the authority of the Bios?

Before civilizations, our tribal ancestors existed inside the authority of the Bios. They were hunters and gatherers, with no central authority. The Bios is the interface between the Cosmos and life, birth into the bios, death into the cosmos. It's a giant experimental lab, the place of evolution, Darwinian ideas of natural and sexual selection. Environmental groups like Green Peace use the authority of the Bios to justify interfering with commercial activities. The ancestors of people who populate our planet evolved in the womb of the Bios. Without nature, man and his authority can't exist.

The Authority of the Demos

The DEMOS is a concept of authority, which comes from people joining together to form a central authority. The common ingredient in all civilizations and societies is a central authority. Without authority we have anarchy and move back into the authority of the Bios. This option appeals to some political thinkers who consider themselves anarchists and like the idea of using the Bios as their source of authority.

Authority motivates people into co-operation; from this perspective, all civilizations are the same in that they have a central authority. The difference between civilizations is the source of their authority. The Chinese Empire, the most enduring civilization, which spans some 5,000 years, has almost exclusively used an individual or ruler as a source of authority. The English language contains dozens of words describing individuals who are used as a source of authority: ruler, emperor, dictator, king, queen, czar, pharaoh, etc.. There is little difference between them.

The second most popular source of authority is a belief system (religion). In our modern day it's not difficult to find a society utilizing a belief system as a source of authority. Iran and Iraq utilize the Koran; some orthodox Christians use the bible. Historians tell us western civilization during the medieval period used the Roman Catholic belief system as a source of authority from the time of Constantine in the fourth century AD, until the Renaissance in the fourteenth century.

The least common source of authority in recorded history is Hellenism, or using the demos or people as a source of authority. Using people, as a source of authority, is the most complicated. It is a relatively new concept beginning in antiquity with what we know of as a Greek City State. Historians tell us Athens and Rome both began as Greek City States; Rome moved towards a representative participatory democracy with its republic while Athens used (participative) democracy. Although using people (democracy) as a source of authority was rarely used in western civilization, it has proven to be the best decision making system we have ever known.

Switzerland used direct democracy at the end of the 13th century, hundreds of years before the USA built its republic. Great Britain and her commonwealth countries gave the common citizen an opportunity to participate through a voting process early in the 20th century. If the per capita income of countries having early democracies is any indication of their success then all nations should be working to increase the democratic aspects of their decision-making authorities.

Most Western nations use some form of representative democracy (participatory democracy) where citizens are given an opportunity to participate in the question of who will hold the authority of their jurisdiction.

Authority is a word commonly used in our modern world as a person or group of people (Committee) responsible for making decisions for components of society:

Health Authority, Education Authority, and Transportation Authority. The concept is entirely man made thus the source of authority comes from the Demos. Governments and industry operate using these extremely complicated mechanisms of annual conventions, boards, committees and subcommittees filled with rules of order and parliamentary procedures. This subletting of authority works but some believe it to be inefficient, self-serving, and fraught with disillusioned sometimes-angry participants who must suffer decisions favoring those with authority. Despite the criticisms, people living in western society have never lived better. With the exception of arms technology, even nations using an individual or belief system as its source of authority benefit from the spin offs of western society.

The Authority of the Ethnos.

Inside every society there is a brewing **ETHNOS**. This is the most destructive level of authority. It can utilize a ruler, a belief system, or people as its source of authority. The ethnos works from within an established jurisdiction, but outside the established political authority causing civil disturbances. A common part of the Ethnos is the savage underground economy of drugs, prostitution, gang warfare, smuggling and political subterfuge. Any normal human activity deemed illegal by the official government will without exception become part of the Ethnos and these laws should be considered an incentive to crime.

Underprivileged people inside a jurisdiction will form groups or gangs. There have been cases where religious groups have replaced the established authority with the authority of a belief system. Often there is a vested interest in the formation of factions in society responding to some inequity. Usually the ethnos responds in kind through civil disturbance; moreover if the ethnos becomes powerful enough to over-throw the existing authority by revolution then the outcome can be a devastating dictatorship or a better society. Human beings love watching the murder and carnage in civil disturbances as evidenced by the popularity of movies and documentaries made using civil disturbance as their subject matter. A few historical examples of the ethnos taking over an established authority are the proletariat and bourgeoisie in the French Revolution, the abolitionist north against the south in the American Civil war, the recent conflict between the Serbs and Croatians in Yugoslavia and the conflict between the Hutus and Tootsies of Uganda.

Ancient history is a chronicle of endless war amongst jurisdictions and civil disturbances within. There is one anomaly. Before democracy the Plains of Attica (ancient Greece) were alive with ethnos with continuing civil disturbances. After the democratic principles of the Citizen's Assembly became the highest authority in the land with the proclamation, by Cleisthenes in 508 BC, no individual could question the authority of the Citizens' Assembly. The noted historian Sir Moses Finlay suggests there was a lack of civil disturbance inside Attica for some 300 years. The foundation for Western Civilization was nurtured in this fertile environment.

There is little threat of revolution or political upheaval caused by the Ethnos (special interest groups) in most modern democracies; however, there is a lot of pain and unhappiness. Because no one knows if decisions made by representative governments are legitimate, (the majority are in favor of the outcome), anyone can oppose the law building a larger ethnos. The cost of controlling the ethnos escalates as our communities move away from democratic political systems. If the trend to erode our democracies continues we should expect to pay more for policing and basic defense.

The Nature of Man.

An individual with no political authority will act like a person with no authority. The individuals will not get involved, they will not contribute, if they can, they will build a fortress around themselves, become reclusive and think the rest of the world is somehow inferior. We need citizens who want to get involved, who feel ownership and have a responsibility for the well being of our planet. If individuals have too much authority they become tyrants, they will feel superior, they will treat people with disrespect and they will use their authority to better themselves while disrespecting the interests of the planet. If a citizen has equal political authority they will get involved, feel ownership and responsibility for the planet and take on the responsibility for the future by working with other citizens to find a plan that will bring the planet into a position of sustainability.

Our representative democracies have not given equal political authority to each citizen and consequently we have seen an escalation of failing economies. The costs of our bureaucracies have exceeded the ability of our citizens to sustain the economy through taxes. Governments have been borrowing to make up the difference and selling public assets to eager politically engineered corporations to fend off bankruptcy. The authority of our democracies is vanishing. If we don't act soon the authority of corporations will have eroded the authority of our democracies and we will move into another type of tyranny.

Mankind is unique in the animal world because we think; we have intelligence, and many of us have conscious rational minds. There have been many theories to answer the question as to where did our intelligence come from and why don't we have any close cousins. Some believe a supreme being gave us this intelligence, as stated in the bible: "God created heaven and earth and made man in his image." Others believe an extraterrestrial being genetically engineered us as demonstrated by the evidence uncovered in Von Daniken's documentary "Chariots of the Gods" and illustrated in the movie, "2001: A Space Odyssey". The less attractive theory comes from reading recorded history and assuming the nature of man hasn't changed much in the last million years of pre-recorded history. If we assume our behavior in recorded history was the same in pre-recorded history, it becomes obvious our intelligence evolved using a subcategory of what Darwin called sexual selection, which we could call selection by war. This concept can be explained using the intricate pattern on the peacock's tail and comparing it to the human mind. The peacock's tail evolved over millions of years as peahens selected their mates based on the beauty of their potential mate's plumage. If a peacock doesn't have a pretty tail it doesn't survive to reproduce. Just as the plumage of the peacock was a major survival strategy, the mental capacity of primates is its predominant survival strategy. If the brains of one tribe can't outsmart the neighboring tribe, in a contest of war, the smaller-brained males will lose the tribal war and they will die before they get a chance to reproduce.

In the simplified version the outcomes of wars between tribal groups were decided on the intelligence and ingenuity of the winning tribes. We also know that man has a propensity to kill the males and take the women and children as slaves. This is also a survival strategy providing breeding females for the predominantly male conquering force. Intelligence would play a large role in who survives and what they looked like. More intelligent victors would select the most beautiful remaining women thus the offspring would be more intelligent and beautiful than the last generation. Remember the people you see around you are the survivors. Trillions died before they could reproduce. The survivors come with a full spectrum of qualities benefiting humanity along with some survival strategies unacceptable in today's world.

The question as to why Homo sapiens have no close cousins and what happened to Neanderthal and Cro-Magnon man is easy to explain if one believes our intelligence came from killing and non-consensual sexual intercourse (murder and rape). We ethnically cleansed them out of existence just as we try to ethnically cleanse human beings who are different in modern times exemplified by the murder of nine million people in the holocaust and twelve million in the Gulags of Siberia. After tribal battles the Homo sapien victors would have non-consensual sex with the Neanderthal or Cro-Magnon women and produce infertile offspring.

The value of a strong ruler who imposed strict discipline on his warriors would obviously be an advantage. The ruler would also be the father of many offspring from the women of the defeated tribes, thus most people today have ancestors who were rulers. According to a BBC documentary on Genghis Khan, one in every 200 people living on the planet today are directly related to Genghis Khan who apparently had sex with the most beautiful girls of each village he conquered. If there is some truth in this theory it also answers the question of why some people seem so malevolent and cruel when they are given authority. This cruel and diabolical intelligence is a survival strategy allowing them to reproduce in great numbers.

In a society that encourages rulers or gives individuals large amounts of authority there will be more carnage: war, civil disturbance, draconian bureaucracy, taxes, formation of lawless ethnos, lack of progress to improve people's quality of life and make it more difficult for the majority to pursue happiness. Democratic societies tend to dilute the amount of authority an individual can hold. It is not difficult to find evidence in modern history to support this assumption by comparing democratic jurisdictions to societies that are burdened with dictators.

Rulers make decisions with questionable authority. One can say their decisions are arbitrary. They do not fit in with what is the perception of the betterment of the overall population and even if these decisions were a benefit to the majority, there would still remain a question in some people's minds. The only way a dictator can survive is to continually put effort into oppressing the masses. Legitimate authority in a democracy can be defined as "authority used to make decisions where it's known that the majority are in favor of the decision."

The Bi-nature of man

Democracy tends to bring out the nurturing side of humanity. Generally, women show more generosity and caring than men; however, it's not hard to find female dictators who shatter this generality. The nurturing side has evolved through a need to co-operate for survival. We consider this the good side of humanity.

Many tribal groups recognize two sides in the nature of their people. The west coast First Nations People recognize the dark side of man. The wild man of the woods and the Tsonoqua, wild woman of the woods exemplify this bi-nature. They have special ceremonies (Hamatsa or red cedar bark ceremony) to help their young men control the power of these spirits in manhood. In our western society there is little recognition and no accepted way of dealing with unacceptable traits such as bullying in our schools and work places. In Western society there is little recognition of the bi-nature of people, instead religious organizations talk of good and evil coming from outside the body. You must find God if you want to be good, and if you don't the devil will take you.

Aristotle, in the 4th century BC, recognized that all men were capable of being rulers. It's as simple as flipping a coin: black on one side filled with oppression and guile, and the other side of the coin is shiny and bright filled with joy, generosity and love. The black side of humanity shows itself when an individual is given too much authority; it also comes when people are oppressed and hate their masters. The bright shiny side, or the love and joy shows when an individual lives in a democratic society where each member shares ownership and responsibility by having equal political authority.

The bi-nature is one of ruler or leader. The ruler takes taxes and resources, liberties, and even life itself thereby creating draconian law. A ruler makes changes in society with questionable authority. Leaders are people who give: of their love, their wisdom, their time, their organizational skills, and makes changes in society with legitimate authority. Athenian society discouraged the ruler and encouraged the concept of leader. The Athenian Citizen's Assembly had the power to banish, for 10 years (ostracize); any member who could not stop demonstrating the characteristics of a ruler. Modern western society has given the ruling side of mankind authority over their more humble counterparts from the organizational unit of the family to the highest government positions. The only arresting feature from a full dictatorship is the thin concept of representative democracy and this can fail under stress as seen when a democracy becomes a dictatorship as demonstrated in Germany before the Second World War.

The Concept of Citizen.

Today few people are not citizens of some jurisdiction or other. Some have duel or multiple citizenships. Citizenship usually implies privilege to a group of people who live in a part of the world. There are different rules attached for different jurisdictions. Participants must obey the laws of their jurisdiction and in return they will have a set of rights and freedoms. It's like being a member of a very large club. In most countries the idea that one citizen is better than another is extinguished with a set of rights and freedoms. All citizens are equal under the law; Apartheid in South Africa was an exception to this rule. When it comes to political authority, all citizens' have equal political authority when an election is in progress. After an election the citizens' political authority is given to the leader of the winning party (President, Premier, or Prime Minister). Citizens have no political authority after the winner of the political contest is decided. They rely solely on the benevolence of the elected ruler and whatever influence they can generate by lobbying or protesting.

Arguments exist that give the individual citizen equal political authority more than once every four yeas. It's obvious some people are more suited in today's world to lead: they have no fear of speaking in public, they can stand on their head without trouble, have a distinctive upside-down appearance, a mind that remembers clichés and bits of history, and they give identity to a group. Before an election we give these individuals hero status and, unfortunately, our authority. Many of our non-elected citizens know far more about public issues and are more capable of thinking rationally; yet this incredible resource is wasted because these quiet citizens are seldom heard as their fear of speaking in public above the loud talking-heads in suits our governments employ to steer the masses, prevents their sensible solutions to problems from coming to fruition, so our societies stumble along making tiny steps forward by trial and error always treading on the edge with the possibility of collapse at any moment. There is no problem with a leader who has good council and what better council is there than the total population.

Why should every citizen have the same amount of political authority from the age of consent until the end of life? If you exist on the planet today, you are special. Your ancestors had the correct traits to survive and reproduce with a fragile connection between generations. Trillions of individuals didn't survive. You have the key to survival locked away in your DNA. From this perspective if you exist, then you are equal. History is filled with stories of gluttonous plutocrats who didn't reproduce, and now a hundred years later there is no trace of their existence. Because you exist in the biosphere of this planet, you are equal and, therefore, the authority to plan your future should be shared equally. Every individual should have exactly the same amount of political authority from the age of consent until death.

Human Traits

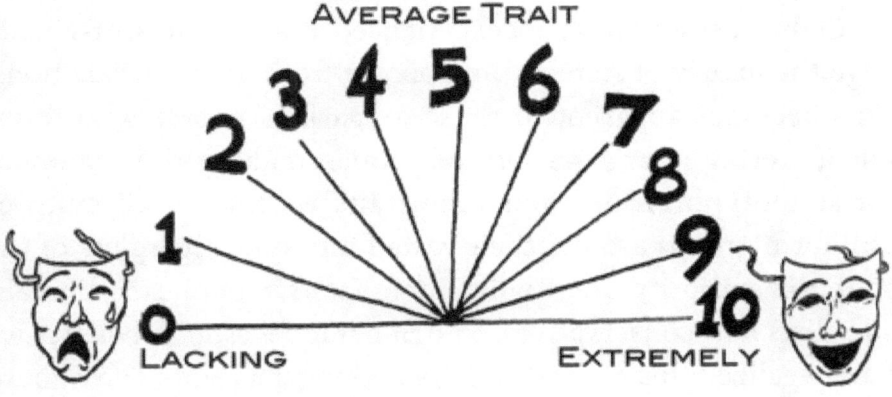

Within a large jurisdiction there is always a full spectrum of all the traits of humanity: the most intelligent to the feeblest minded, funniest to humorless, most evil despot to kindest benevolent ruler. It's wonderful to travel to experience the tastes and flavors of other cultures. It's also fun to note the similarities. It doesn't matter where you are, you can find a group of entertainers in the center of most major cities. The parents of jesters and mimes may disapprove of their children's occupations but somehow the traits their children acquired from their parents draw them to perform among masses of people. These individuals come from all aspects of society and are only the beginning of the similarities you can find in all civilizations. You will find the shopkeepers, the wholesalers, the doctors, nurses and other medical personnel, the builders and trades people, the educators, the lawyers and politicians. Each one of these groups of people has a combination of traits attracting them to the jobs they do well.

People find their specialty, just like the cells in the human body find their specialty as skin cells, liver cells or perhaps some very special cells in the retina of the eye. Like the Khmer Rouge of Cambodia murdering their professional people, if the human body gets rid of the specialist cells in the retina of the eye we go blind and the quality of our life diminishes.

Only those who have not experienced other cultures, first hand, have the luxury of stereotyping people from other jurisdictions. This becomes apparent to those gregarious people who travel encountering a large variety of people, making the argument for stereotyping ridiculous. The traits we find in all cultures will form groups around their vested interests, regardless of the source of authority. There will be democrats, republicans, liberals, socialists and conservatives. In democratic western societies we have legalized this natural activity making it a right (The right to freedom of assembly). We are a whole people; we need every one of these traits and with this knowledge we can better ourselves, and the world we live in.

Our Modern Democracy and the Party System

To attract young people consider the Party System as a system of parties - unending parties where you have fun. Yee Ha! Older hardworking people may like to think of the party system as a system of work parties.

In order to understand how our democracies work, we must understand the decision-making mechanisms within our jurisdiction. Again for simplicity a jurisdiction can be thought of as a group of people. This group can be defined as either the people living inside a demographic area of land, be it a country, state, county, town etc., or it could be a group based on a common interest, a belief system or a life style needing no defined demographic area. Jurisdictions are usually layered, each having authority over established components of society. For example, in a dominion, the federal government having authority over criminal law and fisheries, the state or province having authority over forestry and health, the municipal government having authority over water and sewage. Within each jurisdiction you will find a full spectrum of people.

Our diversity of moral values, our understanding of fair play and honesty shape who we are. I once asked a lawyer friend what he did all day, how could he keep busy when people like myself only see a lawyer for a few minutes a dozen times in their lives. He said; "ninety five percent of the laws are made for five percent of the people, you are not part of that five percent. The five percent that keep me busy are the movers and shakers in society, the entrepreneurs, the politicians, and the people that run this country. These are my clients and they keep me busy from dawn till dusk."

He didn't really say, "you insulted me and you are unimportant riffraff belonging to the lower class of society"; however, based on the increasingly stratified society we see around us there may be some truth in what he did or didn't say. Some people are natural magnates who attract money. If you have money, you have power and privilege with the trickledown spin-off effect improving the quality of life of the lower classes.

This does, however, give an unfair advantage to the five percent who are the ones running our political institutions and heavily influencing our law and policy-making systems. This also puts an unfair burden on taxpayers who must maintain the bureaucracies that make and manage complicated laws, rules and regulations. Obviously, this group is essential just like all the other groups, and if it is based on meritocracy and the benefits outweigh the negative side of a stratified society, then we are on the right track.

The Dynamic of Representative Politics.

People, without any outside encouragement, form groups around their vested interests. A jurisdiction, in a participatory democracy can be thought of as a teardrop on its side. Inside this teardrop is a smaller teardrop; the space between these teardrops represents all the people who don't want to participate. This group has been increasing as evidenced by poor turnouts for elections in which sometimes their numbers have grown to more than 50%. The left side or bulging part of the teardrop represents the poor left wing bleeding heart socialist layabouts. The traits of many poor people often push them away from mainstream society and they find themselves is the left bulge.

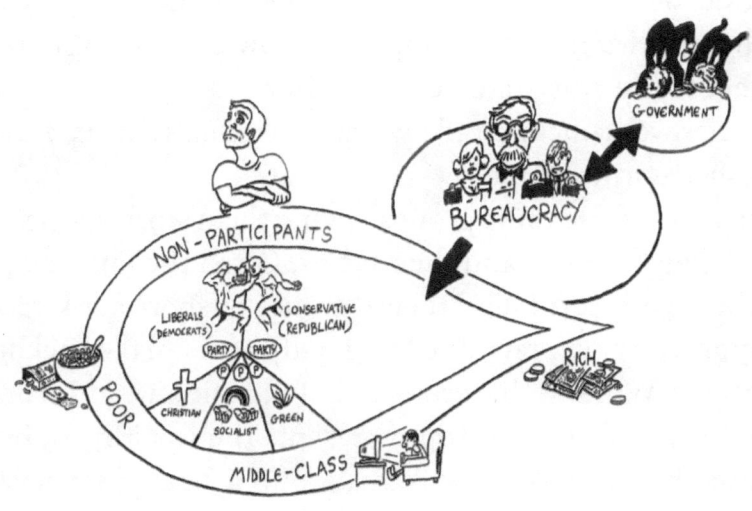

Frequently students, brilliant artists, philosophers and novelists find themselves in the left bulge but more often it's the people who, for what ever reason, are marginalized by our meritocracy. Just as great wealth gives power and authority, poverty and lack of resources gives great vulnerability.

You see these people on the streets. Their hopes and dreams long ago dashed by failure. With psychologically thick skins they pick through the detritus of our society competing with scavenging birds; hunger and comfort their only incentive. One layer up, the young, exploited by pimps and drug lords in a lawless ethnos, burn out their bodies, dreaming of a life that doesn't lead to homelessness. These people rarely participate in elections.

Above them in the millions you find the minimum wage workers, poised on the edge of poverty, a slight sneeze in the economy could find them on the street with no work and no means of support. In good times you can find the marginally poor working three jobs in a desperate act to put their children through school.

Parents dream "The Dream" of poverty-riddled children using their natural abilities to become wealthy. It's rare, but not unheard of for a child born in poverty to become extremely wealthy. In our fickle, democratic, free market economy these stories of rags to riches are wonderful examples of how fair the system is. In a perfect world this statement could be true if our free market economies were uncluttered by monopolies and special favors for established corporations.

The wealthy use these groups, giving them work, in their retail outlets, their factories and their farms. Often the untaxed profits from these enterprises find their way into offshore bank accounts held by greedy plutocrats. The marginally poor are the backbone of our nations. Without this group our civilization would crumble.

The point of the teardrop represents the wealthy, right wing autocrats. It's hard to know if this group is happy; however, the statistics are not good. Living secret lives in controlled estates, rarely venturing out in public, one can only speculate. People who meet them often report their surprise at finding them to be normal, friendly people. If you want to know their troubles the paparazzi and soceity magazines can fill your head with stories and pictures of incredible unhappiness.

Many weathy people try to improve their images through philanthropy, by becoming great heroes of some cause or other. It couldn't be easy, cloistered in a world where you feel jailed by notoriety. It is said that great wealth and power come with great responsibility. Without this group our civilization would crumble.

Both the very poor and the very wealthy have strong influence over our elected oligarchies through advocacy groups. The political lefts have their unions and advocates while the political right have their lobbyists.

The middle of the teardrop represents the hard working, taxpaying, un-represented citizens who don't have the money or time to lobby government. Most of these people are alive with brilliant ideas. Under the oppressive corporate leash they struggle for a sense of self-worth by hurriedly discussing issues of government, industry, sometimes sex, cars and bad bosses all in their ten-minute coffee breaks.

Their days are filled with unending repetition. A career that starts out as fun and fulfilling over decades becomes a burden, burning away their creative energies. Most live in a rut or what's known as their comfort zone. They must work to pay their bills and feed their children. Most feel they have no ownership or responsibility in the decisions made by government.

The middle class watches their family values erode as runaway corporate influence fill their children with sentiment. You can see the middle class walking the busy streets, lonely empty shells, seeking anonymity and finding solace in over consumption. They find it hard to associate with other people with out the help of alcohol or prescribed mind-altering drugs. Living in a chemical haze of caffeine and alcohol and finding little joy in reality they seek the fantasy found on the Internet or Hollywood movies. It's increasingly difficult to stimulate this group into participating when its members know they have no influence or effect on the decisions made by government. Blackberries, i-phones, pagers and schedules dominate their lives separating them from the joys of family and friends. The middle class is the meat in the sandwich between the wealthy and the poor. If you are wealthy you don't need to be a lawyer or engineer. You hire them and use them to control the masses. Without this group our civilization would crumble.

In western society we have all the ingredients for happiness except a say in our governments. We've little or no sense of ownership or responsibility in our communities. Many of us live in fear and ignorance generated by our unrealistic media, successfully spinning small tragedies into earthshaking scenarios of doom, all for the almighty buck. The pursuit of happiness is so exploited by corporations in their attempts to extract wealth from the garden of unhappy citizens; they become blind to their greed and believe the advertising lies they spin.

In the inner teardrop a relatively small number of people form groups around their vested interests creating political parties. People naturally form groups around their vested interests. Some political writers argue that political activity is not natural, that it requires a higher authority to form political parties and legitimate government. From the perspective of an established aristocracy this may be true, but they'd have to argue to demonstrate the United States of America wasn't a legitimate government.

In smaller jurisdictions political parties are not formalized;

however, groups form around candidates representing vested interests.

Within the political party a leader is elected. The leader has great influence, but no more authority than any other card-carrying member. Decisions regarding policy or resolutions to issues are done at the party convention level through a democratic vote. In theory each card-carrying member has exactly the same amount of political authority within the party.

Young people should know that often you can find free booze and food at these parties. The down side is the music sucks and you often have to be quiet when people make long-winded speeches. The decisions made at conventions are considered legitimate because they have the majority of the party members behind them.

Most people in our western civilization know of only one form of democracy - representative democracy (participatory). This is a system where we impose a ruling group of people (oligarchy) upon ourselves for a limited period of time. This oligarchy comes from the political party system. After election the leader of the winning political party becomes a ruler and is the ultimate source of authority for the jurisdiction. The way this oligarchy obtains and maintains this political authority is through a competitive struggle for political support within an electoral process that was established hundreds of years ago. We have no political engineers to build a better system, so we must struggle on with this very inefficient arrangement. It's too bad we don't have a better system because our political authority is very quickly being replaced with the authority of well-engineered corporations.

The Electoral Process.

Today's elections are a game of winners and losers in a representative democracy The laws or legislations produced by government become less important than the personalities of the contestants. The bottom line, if you want to win, is the number of votes cast in your favor must be greater than the opponents. The first step within the political party is the election of a leader. He or she must have the correct charisma, charm and voter appeal and the ability to speak and argue the point for the vested interests of the party members without offending non-committed citizens. Remember half the voters are the opposite sex of the leader so make sure the leader is good looking and has enough sex appeal and voter recognition. Good-looking people are much easier to elect. The party must provide a platform promising logical reasons to elect the candidate. Problems, needs, and issues, common within the electorate must be identified. This platform may have to be changed mid election to accommodate the party's impression of their chances of winning so it should be kept vague and open to interpretation. Researching the history and foibles of the opposing candidates is a necessary ingredient in winning an election. The information gathered should be used to smear the opposition twisting their words and making them appear to be morons by broadcasting propaganda through the media. The political candidates should know the art of not answering questions. When a question is asked they should respond with a question or defer the answer by talking a lot about an entirely different subject. All politicians if they have any intention of winning should be familiar and well practiced in the art of double-speak or bafflegab. Honesty and straight answers is usually a ticket to disaster.

An election committee consisting of Managers of, Research, Publicity, Contact, etc. should be formed. This is where the hard work begins. The first step is to identify support. Known supporters should be handed a voters list and asked to go through the thousands of names identifying possible supporters. The candidate and other representatives of the party begin a systematic door-to-door campaign through the jurisdiction as well as attending all public political gatherings.

The contact committee works on the citizen lists finding prospective supporters and identifying level of support usually by phone. Strong supporters should be given an opportunity to give financially and to help identify other supporters. Undecided and non-supporters should be recorded. Wall charts with each voter's number need to be produced identifying known support.

On voting day scrutinizers working for your party at the polling station record the voters as they vote. Runners deliver these lists to campaign headquarters where each voter is marked off on the chart. After a few hours into the election, known supporters who haven't voted are phoned and reminded that it's voting day. To get voters to the poling place transportation for those without should have it offered by the election committee. Getting your voters out is the most important part of running a successful campaign.

In participatory democracy (representative democracy) the period of time between the date the election is declared, (the writ is dropped) and the day the winner is announced, usually a month or more, is a time when all citizens have exactly the same amount of political authority. The Prime minister and the guy who works in the Quickie Mart each have one vote. When the winner of the political contest is announced the citizen in a representative democracy has no authority. In ancient Athens citizens had exactly the same amount of political authority (participative democracy) from the age of consent until death. Unlike our society there was never a time when the citizen didn't have political authority. This condition existed in Athens for more than 300 years (512BC to 198BC) building the foundation for our modern society.

The election is a competitive struggle between the political parties to win the approval of the most number of participating citizens. After election the leader of the winning political party becomes the ruler of the elected oligarchy. This oligarchy is, by definition, now externalized from the jurisdiction. It no longer requires any approval from the citizens to change laws or enact bills or legislation. In the British Parliamentary System the ruler of the oligarchy, the Prime Minister or Premier, can only be overruled by the Sovereign or appointee of the Sovereign, the Lieutenant Governor. Both positions are largely ceremonial giving an unlimited mandate to the winner of the political contest. The elected official opposition and all other citizens only have influence. All political authority is taken by the winning political party, and given to the leader of the party who then becomes the ruler of the jurisdiction. With very few exceptions, if one adds up the percentage of votes electing the government, the percentage is almost always far less than fifty percent of the population which means more than fifty percent of the citizen in the jurisdiction are not represented by the governing body. Because there is no official way of measuring the quantity of approval from the general citizenship for any decision made, the authority used should be considered questionable authority fuelling ethnos, increasing bureaucracies and government debt.

After being elected a candidate can relax. It's like being a member of a union and you're the boss. Make sure you get a good secretary to answer your mail and perhaps do a bit of work on some sympathetic form letters. For the first two years you can do some pork barreling by looking after the people who paid for your campaign. A year or two before the next election, if you want to get re-elected, it's important to start a smear campaign against your opposition and feel free to use public money to get some media attention. Using money from the public purse have your secretary organize ribbon cuttings and opportunities for pictures of you giving large-in- size small-in-value cheques to pay for necessary public projects.

Most western democracies have some form of direct democracy inherent in its system: Incentives, Propositions, Referendums and Recall processes. These are all crude attempts to involve the general population in decision making. In some cases they do work, and they definitely get the population involved. However, small vested interest groups often exploit these direct democracy initiatives. There is no engineering in the process, and the decisions from these practices are fraught with perils through their wording and timing. The outcomes are often opposite what the majority want, but somehow are now written in stone because the people have spoken.

Questionable Authority

If a government makes rules not knowing if the population is in favor of the decisions they give authority to non-conformists (ethnos) who don't want to co-operate. In our modern democracies it is almost impossible to know if the population is in favor or not. Alternatively the higher the approval rating or the more legitimate government decisions are - the less bureaucracy. With low approval ratings governments form large bureaucracies and need police and armies to enforce their edicts. This expense is added to tax bills and government debt, and has been the downfall of many great nations. At the end of the first decade of the third millennium the leaders of most western democracies and particularly the US and Europe should know they are in the final stage of this phenomena.

In order to increase government approval, it is necessary to utilize the authority of the citizen in decision-making. The less political authority the citizens share the greater the presence of bureaucracy.

The Last Fish Syndrome.

One of the greatest failures of our democracies and our free market economy is the uncontrolled extraction of our natural resources. Part of our survival strategy is competing for food and shelter. If we find something useful in nature, we use it first before someone else does. Our normal response to seeing a fish is to catch it and eat it. If we know there is only one fish left we justify taking it because if we don't someone else will. There is good evidence to suggest our tribal ancestors did not have the same attitude, in fact they had ceremonies to preserve renewable resources. Over thousands of years and many generations, as a group, they developed wisdom. They knew they had to protect the Bios by co-operating or die. In western culture the wisdom of our elders is diluted by our so-called new technology. We don't have the experience or wisdom of generations and because as individuals we have little or no sense of ownership or responsibility in our culture, the last fish syndrome is very quickly using up the biosphere's natural resources.

As western societies close down their industries and export jobs to third world countries where the source of authority is not the people, we survive by selling our non-renewable resources to dictatorships. This is an example of the last fish syndrome. We, the people of western society, know this is wrong and will cause great harm in the future, but we have no sense of ownership or responsibility; therefore, the harm will be done. This is a failure of our political system.

Political Evolution

Civilization has only been on earth for a blink of an eye compared to the natural history of the world. Charles Darwin observed the Bios by describing his theory of natural selection. It's possible to observe the Demos through history, recognizing political patterns of survival. Tribalism, the source of authority being the Bios, was eroded in favor of civilization through the formation of a central authority. This source of authority had many false starts until rulers were firmly in place in Asia and Europe. In western society the belief system of Christianity eroded the Emperor of Rome's authority and for almost a thousand years we used the Roman Catholic Church as our source of Authority. The aristocrats of Europe (Kings and Queens) eroded the authority of the Catholic Church in the early part of the second millennium. Over the centuries pressure on autocratic authority through revolution and protests eroded the ruler source of authority. Participatory democracy (representative democracy) eroded the authority of the aristocracy to give us our Twenty First Century democracies. If we want to survive with the same type of security we enjoy today, we must evolve to the natural next step and embrace participative democracy by truly giving political franchise to our citizens.

Truth

Truth based on sentiment in so many ways controls our world. If enough people know something to be true then we believe, and in our minds it is true. It's not hard to find people who don't believe we are part of the animal kingdom, and it is not hard to find this type of sentiment in the works of our advertisers, our spin-doctors, our politicians and the tall tales told by our friends and neighbors. Keep in mind how bland our lives would be if we only told the truth. Life would be like spaghetti sauce with no oregano, so boring without the spice of embellishment and little white lies.

It is difficult, if not impossible, to find real truth; however, by using the concept of the words **discovery** and **creation** it's possible to sort out what is real truth and just truth created by man. If we assume everything has already been created, then the only thing left is to discover what the Supreme Being created. Scientists discover truth, by using scientific method: they propose theories, set up experiments to test them, then send the methods and results of their experiments to other scientists. If enough other scientists get the same results, the theory becomes truth. As a society based on the consumption of goods produced by corporations, we must ask if corporations discovered what they claim or are they creating claims. The hazard in our modern world is corporations burying the truth because they own the scientists and all their results.

Discoveries are made and with equivocation we can say they are true. The atom bomb is true; the internal combustion engine is true, yet man created none of these scientific discoveries as he has only revealed them. If we assume God created everything, then we can say scientists are closer to God than Priests because scientists seek the truth where as priests create the truth.

Truth in art can be defined as discovering things that are already there. Michael Angelo saw his "David" in the block of marble when it was lying half carved by a different sculptor. He apparently said he discovered his "David" by removing the stone around it. When we read a story or a history we can assume the story was not discovered, man created it. What you're reading now was created by me: therefore, it is, at best, questionable truth.

Western society was built on a concept from Athenian society we call a system of reference. In one of Pericles's speeches he says, "When you speak to the Assembly, you do so at your peril." It was necessary to prove what you said was true, or the citizens could ostracize you and take away your citizenship. Aristotle was one of many who wrote reference books used by the leaders of Athens to prove they were speaking the truth. In scientific literature you will find a bibliography at the end referencing the work to previous known truths.

Science, law, medicine and politics rely on this system of reference to determine truth. Written truth is often a threat to autocrats. China, until recently, has oppressed truth just as the Romans burned the books of Alexandria. It's important to allow freedom of expression to expose truth and allow our world to move toward sustainability. In Western society we have legalized freedom of expression (The right to Freedom of Speech.) One way to find clarity in an issue is open and free debate amongst leaders in our society. This open and free debate must be controlled by truth.

What happened in the past cannot be changed. The problem is, there are as many truths to a story as there are people to tell it. There is only one history, however our scholars have created a written history from the perspective of the victors in great historical conquests. As students we learn the names of hundreds of great warlords: Alexander the Great, Genghis Khan, Augustus Cesar, Mark Anthony, and Adolph Hitler. These histories come from the pens of men employed by the winners, so one would expect them to write favorably about their masters or negatively about their enemies. Written histories are difficult to preserve for long periods because paper turns to powder. After a few hundred years paper histories must be copied. Copies are subject to editing, so it's difficult to tell how accurate the copies are. Much of the history of ancient Greece has been learned from pieces of ceramic pots. As researchers study artifacts such as the dead-sea scrolls, they discover many questions about our modern perception of history. Because the dead-sea scrolls were written between 150 BC and 70AD in Hebrew, Aramaic and Greek on mostly parchment, their meaning is well preserved. These scrolls have exposed many questions about our understanding of the history from this period. Either the interpretation of ancient history is flawed or the people writing the dead-sea scrolls weren't doing an accurate job or as we now accept, "Know your historian before you read his history."

To find the best solutions to problems in our societies we need the truth and the best way to find truth is open and active debate. As citizens we will learn from our mistakes and move towards consensus on the best solutions to problems. Because representative politics is filled with secrecy and unearned political authority the manifestations are often flawed causing increased complexity and bureaucracy.

Trust

Human beings don't trust each other. This is a normal response. Because we have a natural inclination to murder each other, to trust our neighbor would be suicide. We spend huge sums of money on locks and security systems in our homes and businesses to protect ourselves from our own malevolence. In business we don't mind spending large sums of money on lawyers and accountants to ensure honesty and we would rather trust a politician than trust our neighbors to have anything to do with making decisions. The British used this distrust to divide and conquer great nations just as our establishment encourages this distrust to preserve their privileged position. Our world is filled with security systems to protect ourselves from ourselves. The sad thing is this distrust is the biggest thing stopping us from saving the world. In our economic system we have accountants to foster trust and in our political system we need political engineers to account and make fare our political system. With time in a participative democracy human beings will trust each other. We must begin the process of finding this trust soon.

Privilege and Corruption

Western society has always been stratified. From birth we all struggle to put ourselves into a position of privilege. By creating laws, which allow privilege in our society, we remove the fundamental concepts of equal opportunity in the free market economy. If privilege comes with an equal responsibility it is a good thing. When governments issue licenses, regulations, patents, copyright or brand protection it gives and protects privilege effectively creating monopolies. A public body that sets fees and standards must govern monopolies. Corruption in representative government is understandable when the ruler of a jurisdiction holds so much political authority. On one hand governments suffer enormous pressures, from armies of lawyers and lobbyists, to grant privilege without instituting controls over privilege (corruption) allowing individuals, and corporate bodies to legally exploit society without the required responsibility. On the other hand professional people are well recompensed for providing a consistent high quality service to the citizens. Professional people are given privilege, regulated by governments and they pay dearly by educating themselves, working long hours, and being subject to legal policy judging their standard of conduct. The conflict of interest comes from individuals with political power issuing exclusivity to non-entities such as businesses, companies, and corporations The individuals who discover the original idea for a patent rarely get recognition because the company they work for automatically have exclusive rights to anything developed in their company. Business groups harvest the hard work of graduating students who have been educated in public schools and then patent the rights to their employee's ideas. With these monopolies or exclusivity they exploit the masses creating excessive profits, which in turn drain economies. The results of representative democracies granting privilege can be seen in the crumbling economies of Europe and America. Corporate-owned patent protection, copywrite protection, brand protection and legislative privilege are detrimental to the overall population. The frustrating thing is our representative governments don't have the authority or will to make effective change. In a participative democracy there could never be a problem of not having enough political power to make necessary changes because legislative privilege would be earned and controlled by the public thereby eliminating corruption.

If today we can appreciate the wonderful world we live in we must acknowledge who we are and where we came from because tomorrow may be too late to effectively slow down the destruction of our vital biosphere.

The question is: if there is some truth to what we have just read, can we use what we have learned from our history to move towards a better society or should we live in denial believing we are somehow different from our ancestors.

A Clear Plan
(to be revised by a qualified political engineer.)

Can you imagine living in the year 2100 and looking back at the year 2000? If we do the correct things now our descendants might be in a position to consider us politically primitive. You might hear a schoolteacher of the future talking about the injustices of the past just as we currently talk of the lack of democracy for women and landless people and even slavery a century and a half ago. The history books of the future might tell of a time a mere 90 years previously when there was; no right to participate in politics, no right to food and shelter and no right to safe sex and drugs. A time when people were enslaved in the workplace and governments made laws serving the criminal ethnos who supplied prostitutes and drugs at inflated prices to a desperate uneducated public. A time of madness when fabulously wealthy drug lords went to war with established governments and established governments went to war with other countries because of their lust for oil.

Future teachers might have difficulty convincing children how lucky they are because they can walk freely to their unlocked homes and talk to strangers without fear. The children of the future, knowing no other world, would have trouble imagining how their ancestors could have possibly lived in the year 2000 in a world of paranoia, crime and hate.

To change our political systems we need political engineers to update and improve efficiency. Our universities should begin the process of recruiting people with knowledge of political systems immediately. Fundamental principles and a code of ethics should be established using the knowledge of political scientists.

Principles:

- No political decisions can be made unless all citizens have access and exactly the same amount of political authority to apply to the system.
- No individual or group of people can overrule the decisions made by the Citizens' Assembly. .

How many of us understand political principles and forms of government? How many high-ranking politicians, schoolteachers or leaders in our society know anything about the sources of authority in our lives and how important it is to know how politics is used to strengthen the good sources and diminish the negative. One of the most important subjects in ancient Athenian schools was politics. The day after a young man became a citizen at the age of eighteen he was expected to be able to run the Citizens' Assembly.

We need to enlighten our children by teaching political principles in public schools. Every single child reaching the age of consent should understand the principles of authority, the various forms of government (republicanism, parliamentary democracy, dictatorship, Communism, the difference between participatory and participative democracy etc.) and he or she should understand the benefits and limitations of each system. They should know how to establish a legitimate decision in a group by being able to run a dispute resolving mechanism before they become citizens.

They need to know what it means to be a citizen. They should know what their charter of rights and freedoms means and what their responsibilities are if they want to maintain these rights and freedoms. Our schools should foster trust and tolerance between the students and the adults they associate with. The biggest day of a young person's life in the modern world will be the day they become citizens, the day they take on the responsibilities of citizenship and the day they can honestly say they have ownership in their communities. This is the special day when the responsibility for the future of mankind and the biosphere of our planet falls directly into their hands.

There is no need to know the names of past Presidents or Prime ministers. There is a need to know the sequential struggle for rights and freedoms and what these rights and freedoms mean. What is suffrage and how did the people of the past win the right to vote for a representative? Who were the suffragettes and what did they go through to win the right to vote. Believe me the great heroes of the past were not the Prime Ministers or Presidents but the common people who had the courage to stand up to the pawns who ran our governments.

The work of a political engineer

First they would assess our present situation.
- Is there an adequate decision making mechanism in place at the present time?
- Does every citizen have equal political authority?
- Does every citizen have equal access to the decision-making mechanism?
- Does every citizen have freedom of speech and equal access to the media?

- Is there a mechanism to connect citizens to the decision-making system?
- Do citizens have a way of identifying themselves as citizens (proper citizen's cards)?
- Do citizens have a way of monitoring their status and that of whom they have placed their political authority?

These are just a few questions the engineer must answer. If a political engineer from the future was asked the same question about our present political system it would be like asking a civil engineer of today to design all the roads and bridges needed for the city of New York starting in 1800. The bottom line is we've a lot of work to do. In today's world a political engineer would need to be a little crazy to even begin. Only the question, is there an adequate decision making mechanism in place at the present time, would get a bare pass. The engineer might say, yes, a decision-making mechanism is in place, but it is inefficient and needs updating. The engineer would have no authority to do more than recommend changes.

The Role of the Political Engineer.

As society progresses into modern democracy, we will need professional people who can set up mechanisms to obtain the best outcome from our decision-making mechanisms. Just as whole milk naturally stratifies over time, leaving a layer of cholesterol rich fat at the top, groups of people naturally stratify leaving a layer of bosses and bullies at the top. The job of a political engineer is to homogenize political authority giving each citizen the same amount of political authority.

Based on the premise that each citizen has exactly the same amount of political authority political engineers would set up mechanisms to focus this authority. To begin: no decisions from the electronic citizens' government would have political authority. It would be a parallel system until the majority of the citizens felt confident enough to give it authority. In Attica the citizen's assembly had no authority for some 90 years until the citizens gave approval to Cleisthenes's proclamation in 508 BC. After the proclamation was ratified giving the Citizens' Assembly authority decisions made by the citizens' assembly came from the highest authority in the land and no person or group could overrule them.

An example of a decision-making mechanism may look like this:

Search out a public, secure, information system in a jurisdiction. A good choice would be our present lottery system. The lottery system is secure, publicly owned, not connected to the internet and ubiquitous in that each citizen is given equal access:

- Set up a registry of citizens and issue each citizen a proper citizen card capable of accessing the political system.
- Install voting soft ware in the information system.
- Allow citizens to practice using the system to vote for candidates on Election Day while officially using the old method.
- Allow citizens to practice changing which politician they gave their political authority to at anytime.
- Encourage each political party to produce alternate pieces of legislation so citizens can practice moving their support to the opposition if they like its solution better.
- Set up the voting system so citizens can practice voting for alternate pieces of legislation rather than giving their authority to a politician.
- This parallel system would be used and evolved but never have authority until a majority of citizens felt confident enough to make it official.

There is no need to change parliamentary procedure. People form groups around their vested interests. These groups form political parties which compete in a competitive struggle within a jurisdiction for the peoples' approval every four years or so. When the people vote, they chose their representative and decide if they should give that person their political authority in the form of proxy. A feedback mechanism is created through an electronic balloting system. Individuals can give their political authority by proxy to any elected official or take it away and move it to another politician at any time. The successful political party would win because the majority thought it had the best agenda, listened to the people, identified needs or problems, and formed the best plan for upcoming sessions of government. It wouldn't matter which personalities got elected.

The agenda would be published before the secession of government and for each item on the agenda it would include an explanation of the need or problem and an objective that should be reached with the legislation.

Need or problem---??????????---Objective.

Each political party writes legislation as a solution to each item on the agenda. If our present representative democracy truly represents the majority of the people the resulting legislation would be exactly as it is today; however there would be no doubt about the legitimacy of the legislation. If the majority didn't like the government's response, a competitive struggle for the peoples' approval in the house with first second and third readings would take place. Along with criticism of the opposition's solution, each political party would extol the virtues of its own solution. Interested individuals would cast their votes along with the politicians who would use the authority of the citizens who had given their authority by proxy to the politician. The count would take place for first reading. After seeing the results the political parties would be given a set amount of time to reword or change their solutions to make them more palatable to the public. After second reading the process would be repeated and after third reading the chosen legislation would be slotted in between the problem and the objective on the agenda item. This legislation would be the result of the total population participating either through their representative via proxy, or by voting on an individual basis. There would be no question of the legislation's legitimacy.

*Need or problem---***Chosen legislation***---Objective.*

Of course each piece of legislation would produce its own unforeseen consequences. If the consequences were great enough, a political party could win the next election by putting the problems caused by the previous legislation on there electoral agenda and the whole thing would go through the problem solving mechanism again. The end result would be an effective, enduring law that worked.

Clarity and simplicity would be essential if the political party wanted to get the support of the people and concessions to special interest groups would be minimized.

Strengths.

- Solon's reform in 594 and Cleisthenes' reform in 508 BC were intended to create industry and reduce the problems of factions forming in Athens. Participative democracy gave each male over 18 who were not a slave something in common. They had equal autonomy at the citizens' assembly.

The leaders of the factions could further their cause at the assembly if it was legitimate in the eyes of their peers. In this way the interests of minority groups moved toward the majority group and the majority group moved toward the minority group in a process of moving towards consensus. In our modern world every citizen would have a citizen card, which would have exactly the same political value giving each citizen the same amount of political currency. Logic and common sense would prevail. Decisions would not be made because of pressure put on government by lobbyists.

- We would enhance our present government. We now have Democracy 1.0; the new version will be 1.1. Imagine using a 200-year-old system of transportation in our modern world; we would be up to our eyes in horse manure, or using DOS 1.0 today. It works, but man is it is awkward and slow.
- By utilizing the untapped resource, our people, in decision making; we would come up with the best decisions that need little or no bureaucracy or policing to support them.
- Stop minority groups (like unions or corporations) from influencing our governments.
- Give non-political experts in our society the chance to become leaders and make positive change by supplying political parties with the best solutions.
- Give real political power to elected officials rather than just influence in policymaking.
- Participative democracy would make the job of being the people's representative more pleasant and rewarding. Instead of being pawns in a political system, politicians would have a real job of listening, producing solutions, and selling concepts to their constituents. They would earn

the authority, by proxy, of citizens who had confidence in them.

- Citizens with political authority will demand the truth. This will increase integrity in our political leaders. The more integrity and public trust, the more political power a representative will have in the form of proxy. On the one hand in this system an untrustworthy politician who has no support from the electorate would be a lame duck on the other hand if he had the trust of tens of thousands when he lifted his hand to vote in the legislature, he would have the power of tens of thousands of citizens.
- Participative democracy would change the attitude of the people, and politicians, by removing the government's paternalistic attitude and giving the majority a sense of ownership and responsibility.
- This system would utilize the recommendations of the advocates of representative democracy, by retaining a strong, expert minority to lead us. At the same time use the recommendations of the advocates of participative democracy by giving the individual equality in decision-making.
- Today the individual and the state are moving away from each other. Participative democracy bonds the two.
- Participative democracy would remove any chance a decision could be made, not for the betterment of the citizens, but because the winner of a political contest arbitrarily wanted to destroy what the opposition had accomplished in the previous government.
- Governments of today are rapidly loosing authority due to international pressure from corporations. No individual, group, or powerful corporation could question the result of a government with a participative democracy.

- Today everything is about money. Participative democracy would form a new type of currency. In some cases status would be more important than money and no one has enough money to buy status.

What would the political system of the future look like say ten years after people gave themselves equal political authority? There would be no need to change any of our political institutions. Governments would look exactly the same. Politicians would get elected just as they are today. Governments would change about as much as they did when women were given the vote in the early part of the Twentieth Century. The structure of government and the institutions we see today would remain the same. Governments with the British Parliamentary System would have their prime minister, their cabinets their elected officials and their bureaucracies. Governments like the United States would have their constitutional republic with their president's office, their congress, their senate and their bureaucracies. Government business would proceed as it always has. The big change will be found in the attitude of the citizens. The ethnos will shrink, many unreasonable laws will be struck down and new sensible laws will be initiated.

Change would occur in our communities. Citizens would get involved in cleaning up the mess decisions made by representative democracy had left behind. Legislation would be passed fixing problems that our representative democracies are incapable of fixing. Places would be found for homeless people. Laws, judged incentives to crime, would be eliminated effectively removing criminal elements from our society. Legitimate businesses or government agencies would provide substances and comfort to the needy while putting the taxes from these enterprises into research and educational programs. Our free market economy would be improved by government legislation taking away monopolistic privileges given to established corporations in the past. Ultimately, people would be given equal ownership in their places of work, which would eliminate the master slave relationship in the workplace. Real change would come in protecting our environment and reducing our carbon footprint. When things went wrong, people could no longer point a finger and say it's the government's fault; they would only have themselves to blame.

Historical Weaknesses.

- Historically, the people of Athens didn't keep a strong enough armed force to protect their sovereignty.
- In some cases wealth was spread too thin to accomplish large capital projects.
- The failure of Athenians to grant citizenship to immigrants' slaves and women.
- Participative democracy may not happen, because of the unsupported fear mongering of our oligarchies, about tyranny of the majority (TOM). Careful reading of the literature, indicates the cause of negative tyranny of the majority, originates in the vested interest of an ethnos, a ruler, or an oligarchy. History is clear there is no such thing as negative tyranny of the majority in a participative democracy. Many of the aspects of our successful society came directly from the study of Hellenism or Athenian participative democracy which some would characterize as TOM.

Compelling Reasons for Participative Democracy

Our debt is eroding our social programs, our military might, and our people's ability to repay it. Our natural resources are being extracted at an ever-increasing rate, and our social structures are decaying into a new form of lawlessness. The good news is we are standing on the top of a mountain and on the other side are valleys filled with hope and lasting peace. Only the beneficial, sustainable aspects of humanity can fit into this new world by virtue of its system of government.

We live in a representative democracy. There was a reason for this in the past; we were too many individuals and the cost of securing an accurate tally of all the interested peoples votes was too high. A hundred years ago representative democracy worked very well. The majority benefited from the spill over of wealth they produced for the wealthy; we can all be thankful for the society that was built in this way. Our population was divided into few who were well enough informed, and sufficiently educated to make viable political decisions. In today's world at least 80 % of us are educated and probably better informed than the best informed of our forefathers. With Internet, the press, television, and radio, anyone can be just as informed as the leader of the country. We live in the information age.

There are strong arguments for participative democracy documented in dozens of books: such as Benjamin Barber's book <u>Strong Democracy</u> and J. M. Berry's, <u>The Rebirth of Urban Democracy</u>", These two good examples, unfortunately, do not give a clear guide to accomplishing their goal. Each alludes to, but neither state that, representative democracy lacks effective feedback mechanisms while sustainable natural systems abound with feedback mechanisms. Because mankind has, yet evolved through pressure he's put on himself, he must be controlled by feedback from himself. The only feedback nature can offer is annihilation. If one extrapolates into the future of what we call progress, it won't be long before nature has its way and we will be a thing of the past.

Attitudes change. We citizens would feel ownership and responsibility for our government's decisions. People would begin to trust each other. By eliminating laws giving unearned privilege, which are in effect incentives to crime, the need for the escalating expensive new security we see on our computers, our workplaces and our homes would be unnecessary. Healthy co-operation, debate, and participation would ensue. This attitude change is worth billions of dollars in increased efficiency and it would encourage effectiveness in our people. Decisions would be made based on what the total population, guided by leaders in our society, judged to be future consequences of laws. In the words of Jean- Jacques Rousseau, an 18th century French Revolutionary; "man imposes his own freedom", in other words if the majority makes the rules then its members will live within them because they want to. When some one else makes the rules you don't agree with and makes you live within them then you are oppressed.

By utilizing the majority in decision-making we will not only accomplish a sustainable social structure, a sustainable economy, a sustainable environment but also bring peace, brotherhood and goodwill to our fellow citizens.

Examination of jurisdictions in the world reveals a definite relationship between the amount of democracy and the per capita income. The highest per capita income in our world is made by the Swiss probably because they were the first democratic country in the modern world. They managed to avoid participating in the last two world wars. Take a look around, how much democracy does China have, and what is the per capita income? Utilizing the majority in decision-making means more money and a higher quality of life for all people.

Democracy in the Free Market Economy Compared to the Lack of Democracy in Representative Government

It's easy to see how effective a participative democracy will be if we compare the differences between societies where their markets are controlled to societies where their markets are free.

The people don't control the political system in western society. It's almost impossible to get elected if the candidate isn't connected to the wealthy elite corporations or wealthy trade union groups? Our governments are controlled by money and if you want to participate you must have the correct attitude and you must promote the relatively narrow ideals of the true holders of power. .

Before Adam Smith, and other eighteenth century fathers of economics, no one knew what a free market economy was. Aristocrats controlled our economies. Adam Smith advocated a free market giving every man equal opportunity to produce and market goods and services. In our recent history we have good examples of economies that are controlled and economies that are free. The Soviet Union boasted that it had experts to control the production and distribution of goods for its people. The communist oligarchies took away economic authority from their citizens ignoring Adam Smith's ideas regarding equal opportunity in the marketplace. The communists talked about how stable their economy was compared to the out of control free market economy of the west. There's a huge difference between the two ideologies and although there are many problems with the free market economy it has been proven far superior when it comes to production and distribution of goods to the population.

In western societies we have economists who like our political scientists analyze our economies and construct principles of good economic practice. To maintain honesty our economies have accountants who are the backbone of our free market economy.

I would like to equate the communist economic system to our present political system. Both systems, the communist economic system and our participatory democracies practice, from the top down, control of the people with absolute authority. Both systems allow very little input from the people and don't use the individual as a resource. The free market economy is a wonderful example of a participative democracy; we all participate by "voting with our dollar." People control what is on store shelves by selecting the best quality, the best price and, in some cases, where and who made the products. Communist jurisdictions use a controlled economy, manipulated by professionals who apparently have a vast amount of information at their fingertips with which they control production and distribution of goods for their people. Western societies use a controlled political system. Logically, the communist economic system should work much better than the uncontrolled free market economy, just as a representative democracy should work better than a participative democracy. However, it is quite obvious that the opposite is true, at least when it comes to economies. Almost all the surviving communist countries have decided to capture the strength of the individual, handing over control of the market place to their people. China's powerful economy is a direct result of the change from a controlled economy to a somewhat free market economy. Russia has become a democracy that gives privilege and monopolies to special influential people. Their attempt to move towards a free market economy where every person has equal opportunity has been plagued by its discontented ethnos who control the economy with their misbegotten wealth. These plutocrats stifle the initiative of the individual in the same manner our political system stifles the political initiative of potential leaders in a representative political system. We should have an unlimited number of effective leaders in our society not just a few representatives who, for the most part, are elected because of sponsorship from wealthy plutocrats.

The biggest hurdle humankind is faced with today, is the educating of its citizens about politics and allowing them to experience a free political system. People living in a communist country had no experience living in a free market economy. This ignorance made them suspicious and untrusting of western economics. This is the same situation we have in our politics. No one on the planet today has the experience of living in a society where each individual has the same amount of political authority from the age of consent to the end of life. I'm confident if the people of the world had the experience of living in a free political system, they would have no doubt our present political system is barely adequate, just as we now know the communist economic system doesn't work as well as a free market economy. Before we move away from our representative democracy it is absolutely essential we follow the historical example left to us by Solon when he set up a dual system of government in Attica in 600 BC. The Citizen's Assembly had no political authority until the people had ninety years to practice, perfect and achieve confidence in the participative system legitimized by the Citizens' Assembly in 508 BC.

If one examines the good things about Western Societies, one notices a wonderful variety of affordable goods of excellent quality. This is because everyone participates by voting, on what they think is good by buying it. Few producers of goods and services are allowed monopolies? The producers of goods and services must enter into a competitive struggle with other producers. In a free market economy the survival of producers of goods and services depends on choices made by economic citizens. We have effective feedback mechanisms in the free enterprise system today, but our representative governments do not have the will or the authority to maintain a free market economy and our functioning economies therefore are at risk from monopolies and big box stores.

Imbedded Ideologies

Bureaucracy is a form of policing, and as our government becomes more paternalistic we need more bureaucracy. When people make rules for themselves these rules become self-policing and therefore require less bureaucracy. The benefit is greater effectiveness, more money and a higher quality of life for everyone.

We all have an authoritarian attitude, a capacity to make decisions based on the past, and implying the future. Like all things if this skill is not exercised, it will deteriorate and we become apathetic. This apathy is what is necessary to form a strong liberal representative democracy according to Joseph Schumpeter, a well-known political writer in his book, <u>Capitalism, Socialism, and Democracy</u> written in 1943. The electoral mass is incapable of action other than a stampede, ". His theories formed the main political philosophy in the middle of the twentieth century. These theories are readily lapped up by the political institutions of our day. (See article "Wired Democracy") The author warns of instability ensuing if the masses of the lower socio-economic classes exert their destructive powers on society. Schumpeter strongly criticizes the classical theory of democracy, saying it is an eighteenth century theory of people like Rousseau and Mills which represents backward thinking. This man, who has helped shape our democratic institution, didn't realize that democracy is 2500 years old not 200. Schumpeter's question is how can we change the way people think so they will be more apathetic and passive, resulting in a strong representative democracy. This problem was eluded to in the 1995 issue of Time magazine. "HOW ELECTRONIC POPULISM THREATENS TO SHORT-CIRCUIT REPRESENTATIVE GOVERNMENT IN AMERICA." To me the challenge is obvious, change the system to a participative democracy, and reap the rewards.

Our political parties' reason to exist is to get elected. As the electorate becomes better informed they demand more services. The political parties know that to get elected they must provide more services: however, there is a catch 22. Services cost money and in order to provide more services the party must tax the people more. If they tax the people more, they won't get elected.

Some time ago governments figured out a way of providing more services and not increasing taxes. They borrow money on behalf of the electorate, and do everything to hide this debt from the general public. Get elected now - pay later. And why not since elected officials only last on average two terms.

Today people are informed not only about services, but also our debt. What can a representative democracy do? Be courageous, tax the people, and not get elected as the people balk at every turn; then hope that the next government is as courageous as the last, or destabilize society by slashing services to the have-nots so that the haves won't have to pay taxes. The world is in serious difficulty.

We are in this mess because of government's paternalistic attitude to people and the apathetic attitude individuals in society have adopted.

Optimism

There is hope and a reason for optimism. For the last twenty years western democracies have had the technical ability to run an electronic democracy. Today social networking is creating a type of social currency influencing people in authority and organizing masses of people in protest. The struggle for democracy in the Middle East would not be possible without the miracle of electronic connectivity. The next step is political currency where citizens not only wield social influence but they also wield a small amount of political power. There will no longer be a need to march in protest or camp in the middle of cities risking confrontation and violence to bring awareness of the shortcomings of our society. We will all have exactly the same amount of political currency, to be used on a case-by-case basis or transferable to a politician through proxy. When the social influence people are exerting through social networking is changed to authority, political parties will provide options for the people to vote on. Equal political authority will not only shift the attitude of the citizen from oppressed to progressive, but will also change paternalistic pomposity found in today's politicians into a collegial attitude with their fellow citizens. The blame or credit for making decisions will shift from the government to the body of citizens. Responsibility in decision-making will compel people to become less apathetic and more involved. It will also end the secrecy and dishonesty we see in modern politics but the biggest benefit will be the direct link between non-political leaders in our society and the political authority of a participative democracy. When leaders in society such as Dr. David Suzuki or Al Gore fill our heads with facts about what we are doing to the planet we will be in charge of making effective changes to fix the problems we face.

It is only a matter of time before a brilliant young person sees the need for a participative democracy and just as Mark Zuckerberg built Facebook, after he recognized the need for a social network, this person will begin a wave of ownership and responsibility never seen before on the planet. Progression will replace oppression in a new age of anything is possible. Impossible challenges today such as ending homelessness, poverty, the destruction of our environment and the collapse of our economies will be accomplished in the new age.

For millenniums the common man has had little effect on political decision-making. It's like getting enthusiastic about growing a garden, while year after year plants come up only to wither. It's not long before an attitude of, "why bother?" develops. If you have no effect you don't want to put the effort into gardening anymore. However, just as a gardener who grows a beautiful garden has no shortage of energy, an electorate who finds they have autonomy, will have unending energy to find the best solutions to problems.

Questions and Uncertainties

The question remains, if we do utilize our present resources and form a participative electronic democracy, one can only speculate on the outcome. However, one can take comfort in the writings of the leaders of our past.

> Theodore Roosevelt: "The majority of the plain people will day in and day out make fewer mistakes in governing themselves than any smaller body of men will make trying to govern them."

> Thomas Jefferson: " I know of no safe depository of the ultimate power of the society, but the people themselves, and if we think them not enlightened enough to exercise their control with a wholesome discretion, the remedy is not to take it from them, but to inform their discretion."

> John Stewart Mill: "The greatest dangers of democracy lie in the sinister interests of the holders of power."

> Rousseau Jean Jacques: "Man imposes freedom on himself."

Few would argue that modern society exists today because of this ancient anomaly called democracy and the environment of liberty that was created in Athens, a freedom sufficient to allow the scholars of that time to lay the foundation of modern science, medicine, mathematics, philosophy, and politics in a mere 300 years. As always, the powerful have used democracy to their advantage while benefiting the common people through the increased industry and prosperity they have provided. We have a representative democracy today with the view that competition for leadership among elites is the essence of democracy and more important than the laws produced by our governments. Our present prosperity argues favorably for this system. As we enter the information age large cracks are evident in the foundations of our modern democracy. Benjamin Barber a Political Scientist in his book, <u>Strong Democracy</u> describes a growing potential for pathology in our present thin democracy as our young people become disfranchised in a system increasingly favoring the elite minority. I know that there are power centers in the world that would go against a crusade for participative democracy. However I believe participative democracy is inevitable and a reason for hope. We will utilize not only the males over 18 as they did in ancient Greece, but also the females, and we have no slaves to exclude.

Of the dozens of books that have been written on the subject of participative democracy, none have a viable system that will work for a variety of reasons.

- The first reason is history and our individual life experience. We have lived with representative democracy all our lives, never experiencing anything else. People in our society don't know their past. The fact is; there is only one example of participative democracy, which is that of (Athens 508 BC to 197 BC.) Few would argue that without this anomaly our society, for better or worse, wouldn't exist today.

- The Second reason is a failure of our oligarchies to truly hand over real power to the people. In ancient Athens the Citizens' Assembly became the sovereign voice of the state. No one could challenge or alter its decision. The people's decision was final, just as in our modern elections. Until this time the rulers of factions held power in Attica. When this power was truly divided equally between each citizen, by Solon and later Cleisthenes the rulers of the factions lost their power. They became leaders; leaders who couldn't rule using questionable authority because they had to use legitimacy to be effective within the Citizen's Assembly. This assembly maintained many would be rulers as leaders. Socrates, Plato, and Aristotle all had aspirations to rule; however, they earned immortality as great leaders within this system.

- The third reason is size, ninety years ago we couldn't inform interested citizens, and we couldn't accurately tally all the votes. Today, we can get a message to almost everyone in the world within minutes, quicker than the fastest runner across ancient Attica. The world has grown very small, and we now have the equipment to accurately tally all votes with complete security.

Ralph Nadar thinks the superrich can save the world; I think the common people can save the world if they struggle for real political franchise. And let's face it, there just isn't enough money out there even if the superrich cough up everything they have. By utilizing the largest resource we have, the majority of our people in decision making, we will have a chance to slow down our present destructive momentum and create a new world based on the joy of life with our fellow humans, and harmony with all life on this planet. Our leaders need only have the goals of a sustainable economy, social structure, and environment; and then allow the people living in a participative democracy to do the rest.

It is time all people rise up with a call for a new kind of suffrage. It is time we ended the cycle of war and make real progress towards insuring our future. The solution is before you. You can save the world with suffrage.

References

1. Desola Pool, Ithiel <u>Technologies of Freedom</u> Cambridge, Mass.: Harvard University Press. 1983 343.73
2. Finley, M. I. <u>Democracy: Ancient and Modern</u> London: Holgarth Press, 1973 321.8
3. Hanna Arendt <u>The Human Condition,</u> 1958.
4. Pateman, Carole, <u>Participation and Democratic Theory</u> New York: Cambridge University Press, 1970 321.801
5. Fox, P. W. <u>Politics:</u> Canada Seventh Edition, McGraw -Hill Ryerson, 1991 320.971
6. Churchill, Winston. <u>A History of the English Speaking Peoples.</u> 4 Volumes , Mew York: Dodd, Mead 1983 942 CH
7. Barber, Benjamin R. <u>Strong Democracy,</u> Participatory Politics for a New Age Berkeley University of California Press 1984 423.B243 c. 1
8. Schumpeter, J. A. <u>Capitalism, Socialism and Democracy,</u> Geo. Allen & Unwin, London. 1943
9. Samuel Bowles, Herbert Gintis <u>Democracy & Capitalism,</u> Basic Books, Inc. New York 1986
10. Adler Mortimer J. <u>Haves without have-nots</u> Macmillan Publishing Company New York 1991
11. Woodcock George <u>Anarchism and Anarchists</u> Quarry Press, Inc., Kingston, Ontario 1992

12. Miller, James <u>Rousseau: Dreamer of Democracy</u>
    Book Crafters, Inc., Chelsea Michigan. 1984
13. Cross and Woozley <u>Plato's Republic</u> Macmillan Company of
    Canada Toronto. 1964
14. C.E. Robinson <u>HELLAS</u> Beacon Press Boston. 1948
15. Berry, Portney, Thompson <u>The Rebirth of Democracy</u>
    THE BROOKINGS INSTITUTION Washington, D.C.
16. Richard Pipes, <u>Communism A History 2001</u> modern Library
    Edition Copyright 2001 by Richard Pipes
17. Leon P. Baradat, <u>Political Ideologies Their Origins and impact</u>
    Seventh Edition Prentice Hall, Upper Saddle river, New Jersey
    07458.
18. Allan Bloom <u>The Republic of Plato</u> second edition. Basic Books,
    Division of Harper Collins Publishers.
19. Gwynne Dyer, <u>Future Tense The coming world order</u>
    McClelland & Stewart Ltd. The Canadian Publishers Toronto
Ontario.

Book Summary

I admire and applaud the brave crusaders who try to influence, through protests people with authority. Environmental groups such as the David Suzuki Foundation, Green Peace, The Nature Conservancy and social justice groups namely the Occupy Movement bravely struggle to influence authority. These are the true heroes in our society. Numerous excellent documentaries, like Leonardo Dicaprio's 'The Eleventh Hour' and Al Gore's 'An Inconvenient Truth,' point out what will happen to our biosphere if we don't change course. However, when push comes to shove it's all very well to be informed about a problem but in today's world being informed is a useless exercise because individuals have no authority to do anything about it. My thesis offers a possible solution by empowering individuals giving them full citizenship, responsibility, and ownership in these problems. This authority would empower citizens to exercise their authority by demanding truth and expelling ineffectiveness.

Perhaps you've, watched such documentaries, read books or attended lectures about our ancestors to gain a tiny understanding of what it would be like to live in a world where there is no law against manslaughter, nonconsensual sex or genocide. It's not hard to believe that the most dangerous, cunning and cruel creature on the planet is not the shark but mankind. Some say we are nature's knives, put here to reduce the number of species on the planet. We are not only the most dangerous predator on the planet, but also the only predator of our own species. Our very success has come from this complicated survival strategy of killing our fellow man (murder) and having non-consensual sex (rape) to select the most intelligent beauties to reproduce. It's quite natural for the Serbian soldiers to kill the men of a village then lock up the women to be used as sex slaves. Such practices were common for great warriors such as the Ottomans, Genghis Khan and the standard among ancient as well as modern aggressors. The best incentive to fight hard was the sex at the end of the battle. Our political system is our only defense against our potential malevolence. Politics gives us rules protecting ourselves from ourselves. At the beginning of the third millennia the beautiful intelligent people who occupy the biosphere of this planet, the end product of thousands of generations of manslaughter and nonconsensual sex, are responsible for maintaining this law and order. We know if we work together we can save the biosphere and in so doing save thousands of future generations of our own species. The solution to a stable world is inevitable. Are you ready?